Never Let Go

A Companion book to "Never Alone"

A True Story of Faith
and Forgiveness

By

Gayle Garcia

Never Let Go

By

Gayle Garcia

Published By:

ABM Publications
A division of HSBN Publishing.
PO Box 6811, Orange, CA 92868

www.hsbn.pub

ISBN: 978-1-931820-77-6

<u>DEDICATIONS</u>

Thank you all for encouraging me and taking
time out of your already busy lives in order to be
a part of this book.

Fino Garcia
Lucinda Mileski
Bishop Andrew Bills

And as always, Joshua

GAYLE GARCIA

CONTENTS

Forward

This book is for the purpose of directing its readers to the source of peace, insight and comfort (Jesus) that may be needed when dealing with a loved one who is battling addiction. It's short and easy to read. It's not to be viewed as an alternative to Christian counseling, drug rehabilitation facilities or 12 Step Programs, as I believe they are great tools in overcoming addiction, but as a starting point to aid in finding your way at a troubling time. As with many people, I didn't have the resources to enlist the services of counseling and drug and alcohol rehabilitation facilities, and was forced to try to navigate a difficult landscape without any professional intervention. My son and I felt very much on our own in finding answers. As alone as we felt, we were never truly alone. Neither are you. God is with you. He spared my son from any lasting effects that the abuse of drugs and alcohol could have caused, and turned our "out of control", dire circumstances into opportunities for healing and restoration. Please let this book be a sign post to point you in the direction of our Lord, Jesus Christ and allow Him to begin, and complete, the good work He has planned for you.

GAYLE GARCIA

8

Chapter One

<u>Our Story</u>

Excerpts from the book:
Never Alone,
A True Story of Faith and Forgiveness
By Gayle Garcia and Joshua Weber
(Mother and Son)

On May 19, 2011, my son Joshua was arrested for Driving under the Influence. This was just the latest in a string of DUI and other drug and alcohol related arrests and convictions. Due to the California Mandatory Three Strikes Law, Joshua was given a two-year sentence. This was after credit for time served, and other reductions in time. My initial thought was, "Not again". I had been travelling down this road with Joshua for nearly 15 years, beginning when he was a teenager. The stories of those times are harrowing and heartening all at once. What I wasn't prepared for this time around was the healing, sharing, loving and forgiving that we would find along the way. As my son and I corresponded via collect telephone calls and letters, I felt as if something powerful was happening. I wondered, was God moving? For

Mother's Day, 2012, I wrote a short skit for my church using actual wording from letters Joshua had written to me. As the play unfolded, the congregation grew still. At the height of the play, the Mother on one side of the stage dropped to her knees in prayer for her son, and the Son on the opposite side of the stage simultaneously dropped to his knees, while Christ cradled him in His arms. The play came to a close with the last words of a letter from the Mother to the son saying simply, "Love, Mom". For a long moment after the play was finished, the only sound that could be heard was the soft weeping of the audience. Our Senior Pastor took the stage, but was so overcome with emotion that he was unable to speak, and I knew that what *I felt* was happening between Joshua and I was real *and* powerful. God was indeed moving, and the message was clear, "Use this story, use this healing to help others". You see, I had felt very much alone while dealing with my son's struggles with drugs and alcohol. Friends and family both turned away.

It scared and confused them, but Christ remained, and Joshua and I overcame. So with much prompting from the Holy Spirit, and permission from my beautiful son, I wrote a book. I called it "Never Alone" because as I looked back over the journey we shared, I realized that in our darkest moments, when our very lives were threatened and all hope was vanquished, through it all, God was with us. We were never alone.

Here are just two of the stories that Joshua sent me from prison –

June 28th, 2011 – And then Joshua told me about his carrot –

He found it one night at chow. The inmates were given baby carrots as part of their meal. You know, the small peeled ones that come in bags at the grocery store. Well, Joshua happened to find one that still had a bit of green on top. He wondered….."Would it grow?" So he snuck it back to his cell (In jail, even carrots are considered contraband). All the jail cells have a single window in them that are rectangular in shape, about 3 feet long by 6 inches tall, with frosted glass at the top, so no one can see in or out. Joshua was bold enough to ask the "Pill Lady" for one of the small plastic cups they use to hand out pills. When I asked him if she was the jail nurse he said, "Nah... she was just the lady who came around and handed out the pills for the inmates that were on medication". He filled the small cup with water and stood the carrot up in it. Then he placed it in the cell window. He said he wasn't sure if it would grow without dirt. I have to tell you, this simple gesture by my son of trying to bring life to such a desperate place deeply touched my heart. But then, that's Joshua. No matter what his circumstance, he could or would bring something good. Remarkably, with only water and sunlight, the carrot started to grow. It got so big that it became the talk of the tank (the area of the jail where Joshua was being housed with 30 or so other inmates) and Joshua became somewhat of a carrot guru. Other inmates started bringing carrots back from chow, showing them to Joshua and asking him if they would grow (most of the inmates came from such tough, urban backgrounds that they had never grown anything on their own). Sometimes they would have a good one, with a little bit of green on it. Other times he would tell them, "No...that's not a good one. It's gotta have a little life left in it for it to grow". His carrot, well the green, leafy top part of it anyway, grew to be about 6 inches tall, pretty impressive considering it only had light and water to sustain it. He would tell me about his carrot in his letters and in phone conversations. It helped him keep his mind off of all the negative things that surrounded him. I told one of the Pastors at our church about Joshua's carrot. He used it as an object lesson in one of his sermons. Josh too, used the carrot as a point of explaining new life and growth to his fellow inmates. God was using this little carrot to teach us all a simple lesson about His love. With the sun, His son, shining down on us and water, the living water of His Holy Spirit to sustain us, we can grow and thrive anywhere and in any environment. Here is one of the letters I wrote to Joshua, inspired by his carrot.

Oh…by the way….he named the carrot "Carrie".

June 28th, 2011 – in a letter to Joshua I wrote –

Dear Joshua,

I loved your story about the carrot, about new growth. It was really touching. It made me start to cry. I didn't want to cry while I was on the phone with you, but just kept thinking about it after we hung up. I thought to myself, "He didn't have dirt". It made me think of when you were growing up and I couldn't afford to give you the same things that other kids had. It was strange, but I kept thinking, "I wish he had dirt". Who would wish for their child to have dirt, right? But what I was really feeling was that sense of you having to go without. I never wanted you to go without.

I wanted you to have every good thing your heart desired, every chance, every joy, every blessing, and even dirt, so that you could grow a carrot and see new life. New, like the one that is growing on the inside of you. The ground has been tilled, the soil fertilized, the seed planted, and now, growth! May you always have dirt. Love, Mom.

And then after being locked in his cell for 23 hours a day, I received this letter from Joshua. I call it, "Building 16".

In a letter dated August 22, 2011, Joshua wrote to me….

…..I'm still in Building 16. All Bad! I see people that came in after me and leave before me. I wouldn't even care except I can't get visits or canteen (the store). I got nothing coming in 16. I can't cut my fingernails, change my clothes or get a new razor. We have to share shower shoes with the whole 200 man building. They don't even give us

cleaning supplies or full rolls of toilet paper. Oh, and no yard either (going outside). Even the hole (solitary confinement) has more action than 16. Not sure how much more I can stand......

P.S. The Catholic Chaplain stopped by and gave me this old book. It has a picture of a stained glass Jesus on the front so I tore it off and put it in my window. Now when the sunshine comes through I have a stained glass window. It looks pretty cool.

I was deeply touched by Joshua's stained glass Jesus and in response, I wrote this:

If I could lift my eyes to see, enough to find your grace
Then in my window clear and bright would be my Saviors face
His glowing eyes look down with love, fulfilled by sunlit days
Forget me not, oh King of Kings, for I have gone astray

If I could lift my eyes to see before the path was lost
Perhaps my stained glass Jesus would not have paid the cost

For whom He came cannot be me, my value
cannot hold
The beauty of His life cut short, death on the
cross was told

If I could lift my eyes to see the hope that
His face brings
Then glowing in my windowsill, a place
where hope now springs
This stained glass Jesus, Prince of Peace, a
comfort in this place
Of nothingness and broken hearts that run a
losing race

If I could lift my eyes to see, what joy my
soul shall find
For Jesus Christ in faithfulness will ever now
be mine
And so I kneel before the King, dirty floor
beneath my knees
The beauty of my stained glass Jesus shining
down on me.

Joshua was incarcerated for a total of 25 months. In June of 2013 he finally was released. For several weeks leading up to that date, there were threats from the guards to "give him more time…no matter what they had to do", and constant worry that they would make good on those threats. There were questions about what county he would be released from, and what time we should be there to pick him up. He had me send him clothes to wear home. He listed his request in a letter like this – Shirt –T shirt, jeans - new, belt – black, shoes - tennis shoes and underwear - clean. I laughed and thought, "Does he really think I would send him dirty underwear?" I bought a wall decal and placed it in the archway between our living room and family room that said – *There's no place like home* – it was meant expressly for Joshua. I bought a new bedroom set and bedding, curtains and pictures and readied his room. I washed all his clothes that had been boxed up and stored away. I filled his closet and dresser drawers with them.

As I stood back and looked at the completed work, I realized all that was missing was Joshua. At the grocery store the week before his release, I bought extra food so that I could prepare his favorite home cooked meals. He had eaten jail house slop long enough! And then the day arrived. My stomach was in knots as I showered and dressed. My husband and I got into our car and drove the 30 minutes to pick Joshua up. We went to the Visitors Center at the prison, the same place we went to check in for visits while Joshua was locked up. They told us that we needed to wait in the first parking lot, the one we had just driven past. We drove back over to it…and waited…Hours.

He was supposed to be released in the morning. It was after 12 pm before we finally saw the white van, full of now free inmates make its way towards us. I was so anxious and excited that I started to shake. I opened the car door and got out before the van even reached us. I was *so* ready for this. The van pulled up and stopped.

The side door slid open. Several men who weren't my son got out first. I strained to see Joshua. And then there he was, smiling as he stepped out of the van. He only made it halfway to our car before I ran to meet him and wrapped my arms around him. Through tears I said, "Finally". He replied simply and gently, "Don't cry, Mom".

I tried for his sake to put on a brave face. It almost worked. We loaded up his few belongings and drove out of the parking lot. And then, as I had said to Joshua so many times, the prison was nothing more than an image in the rear view mirror, small and powerless. Before us was the road home. We were taking Joshua home, and we all know, there's no place like home.

GAYLE GARCIA

Chapter Two

<u>Parenting Isn't Always The Problem</u>

<u>*Luke 15:11-27*</u>
<u>*The Voice*</u>

11 Once there was this man who had two sons. One day the younger son came to his father and said, "Father, eventually I'm going to inherit my share of your estate. Rather than waiting until you die, I want you to give me my share now." And so the father liquidated assets and divided them. A few days passed and this younger son gathered all his wealth and set off on a journey to a distant land. Once there he wasted everything he owned on wild living. He was broke, a terrible famine struck that land, and he felt desperately hungry and in need. He got a job with one of the locals, who sent him into the fields to feed the pigs. The young man felt so miserably hungry that he wished he could eat the slop the pigs were eating.! Nobody gave him anything. So he had this moment of self-reflection: "What am I doing here? Back home, my father's hired servants have plenty of food. Why am I here starving to death? I'll get up and return to my father, and I'll say, "Father, I have done wrong - wrong against God and against you. I have forfeited any right to be treated like your son, but I'm wondering if you'd treat me as one of your hired servants?"' So he got up and returned to his father. The father looked off in the distance and saw the young man returning. He felt compassion for his son and ran out to him, enfolded him in an embrace, and kissed him. The son said, "Father, I have done a terrible wrong in God's sight and in your sight too. I have forfeited any right to be treated as your son." But the father turned to his servants and said, "Quick! Bring the best robe we have and put it on him. Put a ring on his finger and shoes on his feet. Go get the fattest calf and butcher it. Let's have a feast and celebrate because my son was dead and is alive again. He was lost and has been found." So they had this huge party. Now the man's older son was still out in the fields working. He came home at the end of the day and heard music and dancing. He called on the servants and asked what was going on. The servant said, "Your brother has returned, and your father has butchered the fattest calf to celebrate his safe return".

Did you notice the story in Luke begins with, "Once there was a man with **two** sons"? Obviously, one of the sons stayed home and did what he was supposed to do. The other did not. So was it a parenting issue that caused one son to run away and squander his money? Probably not. It seems more like an issue of a rebellious heart.

In fact, the scriptures (Isaiah 1:2) reference that even God, who is a perfect parent, has a problem with rebellious children. It is a human condition. The best that we can do is teach our children who God is and hold them up in prayer and let them choose which path they will follow. If you didn't raise your children with the knowledge of Christ, it's never too late to start. Our God is the God of second chances. It is His heart's desire that we ALL come to a relationship with him. So ask God for forgiveness for any shortcomings you may have had as a parent (and we all do), and move on. Start with a clean slate. Pray for your loved one, and speak to them about the love of God. Let go of the guilt and begin a new chapter in your life as a parent filled with the love of Christ and empowered by the Holy Spirit. And never give up.

Isaiah 1:2 NIV

Hear me, you heavens! Listen, earth! For the Lord has spoken: "I reared children and brought them up, but they have rebelled against me.

Proverbs 22:6 NKJV

Train up a child in the way he should go, and when he is old he will not depart from it.

We live in a fallen world. The Bible says that we have all sinned and fallen short of God's glory (Romans 3:23). Keep that in mind as you are navigating uncharted waters. Give God the time to work in the life of your loved one, remembering that His grace is for everyone. Stand strong in God's promise that it is His desire that none are lost, and that all come to salvation through Christ. Even if your own faith is new, you can extend God's love to your loved one and let them see how your heart and life have been changed. God is faithful. Nothing we do for Him returns void (Isaiah 55:11). Words given in a time of need, deeds done in kindness, for the Glory of God, will have an impact, even though it might not seem like it at the time.

Chapter Three

It's Not Too Late

Genesis 1:3-5 KJV

And God said, "Let there be light. And God saw the light, that it was good: and God divided the light from the darkness. And God called the light Day, and the darkness he called Night. And the evening and the morning were the first day.

It's never too late to change, or to help your child change. If your children were not educated about God when they were young, don't let that worry you. God is not held by time. Rather, He is the author of it. The scripture above speaks about God calling light into being and separating the light and the darkness into day and night. He set the seasons and the years. He has breathed eternity into our hearts. At one point, to save His chosen people and insure their victory over their enemy, he stopped the sun and the moon in the sky. Surely He is capable of reaching into the past and healing it. Surely He is capable of laying out a new future before us. He is the God of the past, present and future. Lift your loved ones to

Him in prayer. Ask Him to redeem the past so that it does not hold you back in the future. Let it be a story to tell as a means of helping others to see how far you have come, not an open wound, or a scar that cripples and keeps you from your God given destiny. Give Him your present circumstance and watch Him turn it into a better day. Pray for His goodness over your future. He has great plans for you.

Genesis 1:14 NIV
And God said, "Let there be lights in the vault of the sky to separate the day from the night, and let them serve as signs to mark sacred times, and days and years.."

Ecclesiastes 3:11 NIV
He has made everything beautiful in its time. He has also set eternity in the human heart; yet no one can fathom what God has done from beginning to end.

Joshua 10:13 NIV
So the sun stood still, and the moon stopped, till the nation avenged itself on its enemies, as it is written in the Book of Jashar.

Chapter Four

How To Pray For The Prodigal

Proverbs 28:9 NIV

If anyone turns a deaf ear to my instruction, even their prayers are detestable.

Matthew 6:5-6 NIV

And when you pray, do not be like the hypocrites, for they love to pray standing in the synagogues and on the street corners to be seen by others. Truly I tell you, they have received their reward in full. 6 But When you pray, go into your room, close the door and pray to your Father, who is unseen. Then your Father, who sees what is done in secret, will reward you.

As you learn to pray, also begin to work on becoming obedient to God. God can bless you no matter what your attitude, but as any parent knows, blessing an obedient child makes more sense than blessing one who is in rebellion. Obedience to God also helps keep us from adding difficulties to our circumstance. Learn His word. You can't share His word in times of need or act on it if you don't know it. Ask for forgiveness. We all feel so much better when we have been washed clean. Seek Godly council. God often uses others to enlighten and encourage us. Serve others. God loves a cheerful giver. Share His love. The more you press into God, the more He will bless you in return. It's His nature and His desire to extend blessings and love to His children. The blessings and love can come in many forms – a quiet night, a shared smile, or even a bit of extra money in a time of need. God is faithful. When you begin to walk with Him and choose His will, you will see His life changing power evidenced in your life.

Philippians 4:6 NIV
Don't be anxious about anything, but in every situation, by prayer and petition, with thanksgiving, present your requests to God.

While Jesus was here on earth, He gave us an example of how we should pray. This example is called, "The Lord's Prayer"

Matthew 6:9-13 KJV
The Lord's Prayer
Our Father in Heaven, hallowed be your name – (Shows respect for who we are speaking to)

Your kingdom come, your will be done on earth as it is in heaven – (shows submission to God's will)
Give us this day our daily bread – (meet our needs)
And forgive us our debts – (forgive us of our sins)
As we forgive our debtors – (help us to forgive others)
And lead us not into temptation – (guard our path)
But deliver us from the evil one – (take away the enemy's ability to impact our lives)
For to you is the power and the glory forever – (acknowledge God's greatness and give Him honor)
Amen – (meaning "so be it")

Psalm 35:13 NIV
Yet when they were ill, I put on sackcloth and humbled myself with fasting. When my prayers returned to me unanswered.

Joel 2:12 NIV
"Even now," declares the Lord, "return to me with all your heart, with fasting and weeping and mourning".

Along with prayer, fasting is a powerful tool to use against the enemy. The Bible teaches that it is a way to humble ourselves (Psalm 35:13) before the Lord and a way to come before Him (Joel 2:12). It doesn't have to be an extreme fast. Three days of liquids without eating solid foods is a good way to fast. If you have health issues that could be impacted by fasting, be wise about that. Think about giving up one specific item from your diet. An example might be bread or desserts, and of course, talk to God and ask for clarity from Him on how you should fast. Keep in mind that He is a loving parent who does not wish to harm His children.

Chapter Five

Worship Breaks Through

Luke 19:40 NIV

"I tell you," he replied, "if they keep quiet, the stones will cry out."

John 4:24 NASB

God is spirit, and those who worship Him must worship Him in spirit and in truth.

Worship is a requirement, not an option. God is so worthy of worship that the Bible tells us (Luke 19:14) that if we keep quiet, "the stones will cry out". The enemy of our faith was cast out of heaven because he wanted to be God. He wanted to be worshipped. The last thing he wants is for us to worship God. He intentionally tries to trip us up with attacks in every area of our lives, from our finances to our children. It makes him happy to silence us. We need to refuse to give up or give in. God is worthy of worship even (and especially) in the hard times. Worship ushers in the presence of God. It gives him the opportunity to break strongholds that may have otherwise taken years to overcome.

Worship in your home and in your car. Carry an attitude of praise and gratitude with you, believing that God will see you through the storms of life. Even in difficult circumstances, as believers we are still God's much loved children, we still have heaven to look forward to and we are still forgiven. For that alone, God deserves to be praised. Be grateful every day for God's goodness, but also be grateful for the hard times. The struggles teach us, and bring us closer to God. They give Him an opportunity to move in our lives and to show His power. Be grateful for the good times, too. They are God's gift to us. Worship and watch God break through with His Holy Spirit and His power. The veil will be torn back, the enemy will be vanquished and we will see (in the Spirit) and hear from God.

Chapter Six

<u>Tough Love, Tender Love</u>

In dealing with Joshua's addiction, I found it difficult to discern when he really needed me and when he was simply trying to manipulate me to further his addictive behavior. God's word has promised a "Helper" (the Holy Spirit) to teach us what to pray for and to intercede before the Father on our behalf. The Holy Spirit also gives us the gift of insight and can help us get clarity on what our next course of action might be.

<u>*Romans 8:26 NIV*</u>
In the same way, the Spirit helps in our weakness. We do not know what we ought to pray for, but the Spirit Himself intercedes for us through wordless groans.

<u>*Acts 1:8 NIV*</u>
But you will receive power when the Holy Spirit comes on you; and you will be my witnesses in Jerusalem, and in all Judea and Samaria, and to the ends of the earth.

The Holy Spirit is not something we are born with the ability to tap into. It is something that God gives. You can ask to receive the Holy Spirit and when it comes upon you, you will receive power from its presence. It will help you by revealing things that cannot be seen by human means, but rather, in a spiritual sense.

Acts 2:38 NIV

Peter replied, "Repent and be baptized, every one of you, in the name of Jesus Christ for the forgiveness of sins. And you will receive the gift of the Holy Spirit".

Acts 19:6 NIV

When Paul placed his hands on them, the Holy Spirit came on them, and they spoke in tongues and prophesied.

John 14:16-18 NIV

And I will ask the Father, and he will give you another advocate to help you and be with you forever The Spirit of truth. The world cannot accept him, because it neither sees him nor knows him. But you know him, for he will live with you and will be in you. I will not leave you as orphans; I will come to you.

John 16:13 NIV

"But when the Spirit of truth, comes, he will guide you into the truth. He will not speak on his own; he will speak only what he hears, and he will tell you what is yet to come".

In going through my own personal struggles, I found the scriptures regarding the Holy Spirit to be true. Without the help and insight I received from the Holy Spirit, I would not have known how to handle all the different situations and circumstances that presented themselves.

From one day to the next, it seemed, I had to decide whether or not to extend mercy and tenderness, or tough love. Should I run to Joshua in his place of need, or turn my back on him and leave him to figure things out on his own?

Middle of the night phone calls, pleading, and crying had become a part of the norm, as did arguments, and cruel words. I ended up so exhausted that I finally found myself on my knees before the Lord. I cried out for His presence and wisdom. I fasted and prayed. And I grew in knowledge and insight. I fell in love with God's word. It was saving our lives! I changed my behaviors, all because of the power of the Holy Spirit. God raised me up and I was no longer twisted and spun by every turn of events. And when Josh saw the change in me, he began to change too (Although at the time he didn't understand why I was so different). So ask God to empower you with His Holy Spirit. He has provided it to us for the purpose of helping us with ministry, whether it be to members of our own family, or the greater population in general. Have the Pastors and members of your church lay hands on you and ask for the Holy Spirit to come and dwell within you. And in a moment of need or confusion, call out to God and ask for the Holy Spirit to provide you with the truth so that you will know how to proceed. Never doubt God's ability to give us what we need precisely when we need it.

Chapter Seven

Proclaiming God's Promises

Isaiah 55:10-11 NIV

As the rain and the snow come down from heaven, and do not return to it without watering the earth and making it bud and flourish, so that it yields seed for the sewer and bread for the eater, as is my word that goes out from my mouth: It will not return void.

Speak to your family, your friends and your children about the ways of God. Tell them what He is doing in your life. Memorize the scriptures and speak them into the life of the prodigal. Even if it seems like they are not listening, even if they respond in a negative or angry way, speak it. Do it gently and in love, use a soft voice if that is the only way you can reach them, but speak it regardless. Your words may be the only Jesus they ever hear about. Your words may be the only barrier between them and an eternity spent in hell. And your words WILL MAKE A DIFFERENCE! You might see immediate results or you may never know the difference you have made. That's ok. God is faithful and He will use our efforts to do His will in reaching, impacting and changing our world. And if need be, He will do it one person, one prodigal at a time.

Chapter Eight

Forgiveness and Joy

Matthew 6:15 NIV

But if you do not forgive others their sins, your Father will not forgive your sins.

Luke 6:37 NIV

Do not judge, and you will not be judged. Do not condemn and you will not be condemned. Forgive and you will be forgiven.

Forgiveness was one of the most powerful lessons I learned from my time of dealing with Joshua's addiction. Truthfully, I wasn't even aware that I was holding on to any resentment towards him. It wasn't until God pointed it out to me that I realized I was holding on to unforgiveness. I was angry that Joshua had lied to me so many times. I was hurt that he had let me down by not becoming everything I knew he could be. I had negative feelings towards him that were affecting the way I communicated with him. I realized that if Joshua were ever going to be healed, I had to get over my hurt and anger and forgive him. Otherwise, I was holding

Joshua in a place of disdain. He would feel that, and his recovery would that much more difficult.

I remember sitting on the edge of my bed crying as the unresolved pain poured out of me. I let it bubble up to the surface so I could begin to release it. I knew that God would demand that of me. His word says very clearly that we must forgive and then it tells us why we need to do so. As He extends forgiveness to us, we must extend it to others. There is no justice in being given a gift that we are not, in turn, willing to offer.

Once I began working on the unforgiveness I had in my heart, my attitude began to change. I could talk to Joshua in a gentler way with no hidden animosity. I noticed that his responses to me were changing as well, and like the scripture says, when I forgave, I was also forgiven. The relationship I had with my son was improving in leaps and bounds and in ways I could only have dreamed. It was amazing how my obedience was the direct cause of a new found joy.

Psalm 30:5 NIV

For His anger lasts only a moment, but His favor lasts a lifetime; weeping may stay for the night, but rejoicing comes in the morning.

Psalm 30:11 NIV

You turned my wailing into dancing; you removed my sackcloth and clothed me with joy.

Romans 12:12 NIV

Be joyful in hope, patient in affliction, faithful in prayer.

And speaking of joy…throughout all of my difficulties, I looked for joy. I knew that God's word promised joy, so around every corner, I searched for it. I found it in precious moments where I least expected it. I tried to offer it to Joshua by means of laughter and light heartedness. Sometimes I would tell silly jokes just to make him smile. Between the shadows, joy would come like a splinter of light and pierce the darkness. It was God's provision for us and His promise to us that He kept as consistently as the dawn of each new day. Praise His name forever!!!!

GAYLE GARCIA

Chapter Nine

<u>Believing In Hope!</u>

<u>1 Corinthians 12:12 NIV</u>
For now we see only a reflection as in a mirror; then we shall see fact to face. Now I know in part; then I shall know fully, even as I am fully known.

<u>Jeremiah 12:11 NIV</u>
For I know the plans I have for you, "Declares the Lord," plans to prosper you and not harm you, plans to give you hope and a future.

<u>Ephesians 1:3 NIV</u>
Praise be to the God and Father of our Lord Jesus Christ, who has blessed us in the heavenly realms with every spiritual blessing in Christ.

Again, never give up. We don't know the full story or what the eventual outcome will be. We only get a small glimpse of what God is doing on our behalf. As an example, let me tell you the story of my favorite Aunt. Her name was Helen. She was raised in a rough environment. Beatings were the way that discipline was handed out. As a young woman, her oldest child was unfairly removed from her care by her own Mother. And then as a young man, that child was tragically killed in a motorcycle accident..

Because of my Aunt's self-destructive behavior, every relationship she had, she lost. Heartbreak was with her every step of the way. Yet there was something unexplainably joyful in her countenance. She could always made us smile (God's gift to her I suppose).

In middle age she was diagnosed with cancer. She knew she was going to die. At the end of her life, a pastor visited her every day in her hospital room (he was probably guided by the Holy Spirit). Every day my Aunt would tell him (using bad language) to "Get Out!", until the day she didn't. That day, she let the pastor come in, and that day, she accepted Christ as her Lord and Savior. Shortly thereafter my Aunt Helen died. She went to spend eternity with Jesus. Now when it's my time to go home to Jesus, I will see her again. The thought of that does my heart good. So never give up hope. My Aunt was saved at the very last minute, the 11th hour! Never stop praying. God has promised us good. He has written about it in heavenly realms. As long as there is breath, there is hope of our loved ones finding Salvation.

Honestly, I thought that I would have buried my son by now. But God was stronger. He was stronger than the addiction, stronger than prison, stronger than anything that threatened our lives. He showed up in a mighty way. He healed and restored our relationship. And He desires to do the same for you.

Chapter Ten

<u>In Conclusion</u>

<u>*Isaiah 41:18 NIV*</u>

I will make rivers flow on barren heights, and springs within the valleys. I will turn the desert into pools of water, and the parched ground into springs.

<u>*Isaiah 35:6 NIV*</u>

Then will the lame leap like a deer, and the mute tongue shout for joy. Water will gush forth in the wilderness and streams in the desert.

<u>*Isaiah 43:19 NIV*</u>

See, I am doing a new thing! Now it springs up; do you not perceive it? I am making a way in the wilderness and streams in the wasteland.

In conclusion I would like to say this… If you feel as if you have reached the end of your rope and there is no way out, if you feel that all of your resources have been exhausted and there is nowhere left to turn, that is just the time for God to show up. In a moment, He can provide a pathway out or an unexpected provision that can send you on your way to a new beginning.

Trust God. He can make something out of nothing and streams in the desert.

Love Gayle

4

Inspirational Messages of Wisdom

Chapter 11

"Beach Glass"

James 1:2 - *Consider it pure joy my brothers and sisters whenever you encounter trials of many kinds.*

I never liked this scripture. I knew it was God's word and I knew that I was supposed to believe and follow all of the scriptures, but this one never made any sense to me. I didn't want to be happy about trial of many kinds. I wanted to fight them kicking and screaming!!! And then I began my 15 year journey with my son trying to help him with his problem with addiction.

I thought that I would bury my son, but God was stronger. I thought that prison would destroy my son, but God knew better and it was the very thing that began to set him free –

There were trials of many kinds. I did not consider any of them as joy. And then God began to work

God began to change me. By virtue of changing me, Joshua began to change too.

Spending a day at the beach with my husband once, I combed the shore for beach glass to add to my small collection. Beach glass is the rounded, worn pieces of glass that the surf, sand and wind have turned into beautiful, smooth pieces of art. There were plenty of shells and rocks, but no beach glass. The pieces of glass that I did find weren't works of art at all. They were sharp and jagged. They would be very dangerous if stepped on with bare feet. I picked them up and threw them in the trash. Those pieces of glass started me thinking... the difference between them and the beach glass that I was seeking was this...The waves, the rocks and the wind hadn't worn them down yet, or softened their sharp, dangerous edges. They hadn't been tossed and pounded enough to have been smoothed out and turned into works of art, similar to the storms of life, that change, reshape and often times teach and mellow us. The storms, the trials of many kinds can make us pliable and able for God to use us.

Now let me finish the rest of the scripture of *James 1:2* by adding verses *3 and 4*

Consider it pure joy my brothers and sisters whenever you encounter trials of many kinds...BECAUSE you know that the testing of your faith produces perseverance. Let perseverance finish its work so that you may be mature *(not childish and selfish) and complete (whole), <u>not</u> <u>lacking anything</u>.*

For me, that sounds like a good place to be. And so I have learned to "consider it all joy" whenever I encounter trials of many kinds. You see, like the beach glass, my sharp edges are being worn away, I am no longer potentially harmful to those around me. I am becoming a work of art, the way God intended me to be.

Whatever it is you may be facing today, give it to God let him use it to heal, change and mold you into his masterpiece.

GAYLE GARCIA

Chapter 12

"Don't Forget The Joy"

Standing by Joshua during his years of addiction, it looked like very different things at different times. Not every conversation I had with my son was centered on his addiction. Very often I would just spend time with him as Mother and Son, chatting about everyday things. Joshua loves everyday things. Many of the letters I sent to him while he was incarcerated, and which are included in my book were about my garden, or what our goofy animals were doing that made me laugh. In my mind, life is made up of the little bits of joy that God give us along the way. Things that come in the midst of the trials to lift our heads. I tried to take every opportunity to find reasons to laugh with Joshua. It was my way of reminding him God's truth about joy.

Romans 12:12 - *Be joyful in hope, patient in affliction, faithful in prayer.*

Psalm 30:5 - *For His anger lasts only a moment, but His favor lasts a lifetime; weeping may stay for the night, but rejoicing comes in the morning.*

Psalm 30:11 - *You turned my wailing into dancing; you removed my sackcloth and clothed me with joy.*

God wants us to be happy. He gave instructions to us to be joyful. His word said that HIS JOY will come! Live in that truth. Believe in it even when circumstances say otherwise

Chapter 13

"Loving Beyond The Pain"

1 Peter 1:22-24 - *Now that you have purified yourselves by obeying the truth so that you have sincere love for each other, love one another deeply, from the heart. For you have been born again, not of perishable seed, but of imperishable, through the living and enduring word of God*

1 Peter 4:8 Above all, love each other deeply, because love covers over a multitude of sins.

And wow, don't our prodigals know how to sin? The pain that is caused by their sins impact on us can be devastating and if we're honest, can make us really mad. I know I sure felt that way! I was very wrapped up in how my son's behavior was affecting ME. How it was hurting ME. And it genuinely was. Then God began to speak to me. He spoke to me through his word, through friends, through the still soft voice of the Holy Spirit. He was showing me that focusing on *my* feelings was not going to help my son. It was going to hold me hostage to his sin. The Bible says that I am not a hostage of sin. *(for whom the son has set free is free indeed – John 8:36).*

The problem was, how could I move forward out of those feelings? I couldn't. Not on my own. But In *Philippians 4:13*, it says *I can do all things through Christ[a] who strengthens me.*

So I asked God to help me. Every day. I whispered it under my breath as I drove to work. I lay away at night, tears running down my face, asking God to help me help my son. And something began to happen. The more I prayed, the more I felt God's presence and heard his voice, the less I felt my own pain. God was moving. He was healing me. As I began to feel God's presence, I began to desire to press in further. I desired to obey, to do everything I could to pursue God. I was hungry for his presence. I desired to see his face. God was teaching me how a real parent loves his children by showing me the depth of His love for me! The result of which, was a change in my ability to process the pain that I was feeling over Joshua's behavior and to have a love for my son that was bigger than my own pain. I began to trust and believe that God really did have both Joshua's and my best interest at heart. It was as if I was elevated above my circumstance and could see beyond the immediate. It was also helping me to express genuine love to Joshua.

The overwhelming love that I was learning from God was growing within me. I was no longer reacting out of hurt or frustration or anger the way I had been, but began to see every situation that I encountered as an opportunity to use firm, strong, rational love to help direct my son's path.

This was not a weak kind of love that allowed him to pull on my heart strings and to manipulate me. And let's be real, our prodigals often times are very good at manipulation. This new love that was growing on the inside of me was strong and determined and capable of making the tough decisions that were meant to work as ways to teach my son what was acceptable, correct behavior and what was not. It became clear that with Christ, I was more than up to the task. That I could love deeply, and that my love for my son could cover, could handle any sin he threw my way. You see, I have been born again, and no longer conform to the world. My God makes me able.

GAYLE GARCIA

Chapter 14

"Never Underestimate Your Faith Journey"

Mark 15:15 - *He said to them, "Go into all the world and preach the gospel to all creation.*

Matthew 28:19 – *Go then and make disciples of all nations, giving them baptism in the name of the Father and of the Son and of the Holy Spirit.*

If we are Christians, if we have been saved by grace and accepted Christ as our Lord and Savior then we are called to tell others about him. Are you wondering if you're qualified? Well, do you have a story to tell of how Christ redeemed you? That qualifies you. Think back on your personal journey. How and when did God get your attention? Who did he use to communicate his grace and forgiveness to you? I'm here now talking to you because of what God did for me. You're relating to it because some of you were in the same situations as my son Joshua. Some of you had parents who were praying for you as I was my son. Some of you are the praying parent. So when I speak, you recognize part of your journey and it gives you hope because you see that I am on the other side of the struggle. Joshua and I have beat the giant. It encourages you. Right now, someone out there somewhere is experiencing something similar to what you are going through and God is likely setting things in motion, even now, for you to have an opportunity to share what God has done for you, with them.

Luke 8:39 - *Return home and tell how much God has done for you." So the man went away and told all over town how much Jesus had done for him.*

This scripture speaks of returning to where you once were to tell how much God has done for you. To let people who are from your country, your city, your neighborhood, or maybe even your tribe, as they called it in Bible times, know what God has done for you.

I have personally often felt unqualified to talk to people about Christ. I get more wrong then I ever get right in life, but that's the beauty of it! You don't have to get everything right, because it's not about you. We're not sharing about ourselves. We're sharing about God and God gets it right 100% of the time!

Do you remember what it felt like to be a slave to sin? I do. I wasn't addicted to drugs, but I had other issues. I was angry, I had a negative attitude. I was temperamental and always wanted my own way. Very immature. Then Christ found me. He redeemed me. He healed me. He gave me joy and faith and hope! I'm not a slave to sin anymore. I am free. Some of you out there know exactly what I mean! I am by no means perfect, but I am covered by grace and learning more everyday about the giver of grace, who is Jesus Christ.

John 8:36 – *Whom the son (Jesus) has set free, is free indeed.*

Below are some examples of Redeemed Bible Characters -

Mary Magdalene – woman with a bad reputation – follower of Jesus.

 Apostle Paul – murdered Christians – wrote most of the new testament.

King David – murderer – man after God's own heart.

Joseph – slave/prisoner – became 2nd in command over Egypt.

Thief on the cross – thief - forgiven.

If God has redeemed you, regardless of your past, you are qualified to spread the good news of Christ Jesus. The Bible states that all have sinned and fallen short of God's glory. We are all on equal ground with none better than the other.

Romans 10:17 – *So faith comes from hearing, that is, hearing the Good News about Christ.*

To help others find their freedom, you must share with them the "Faith Journey" that led you to your freedom. If they never hear, they may never be able to find their faith and be set free.

That being said, never underestimate your own faith journey. Share how God has redeemed you. Don't glorify your past sin, rather, give glory to God for having saved you from it.

In conclusion – Get to know God and understand his great love for you. – (read His Word, worship Him and regularly attend a Bible based church).

Continue to pursue God and His presence.

Pray for His strength to sustain you.

Extend His love to others.

And never let go.

Love, Gayle

About The Author

Gayle Garcia has worked in the Creative Arts Ministry for many years as a recording artist, worship leader, and playwright. It was not until her faith was tested through the harrowing journey of helping her son become free of addiction to drugs and alcohol that her writing turned towards this very personal story.

Gayle now speaks to various groups and shares her story of the trials faced, and the lessons learned during her son's recovery. Her life is now dedicated to encouraging others facing seemingly insurmountable circumstances. Through the healing POWER of God's love, and the confidence in believing that God is faithful, Gayle inspires us all.

To contact Gayle about speaking engagements or interviews, or to purchase the book in quantities for group workshops, please visit:

www.gaylegarcia.com